Calligraphy Basics from Left Handed Calligraphers

Easy and Best Calligraphy Samples for Lefties

© 2021 All rights reserved

Table of Content

Introduction

Lettering and calligraphy are quickly becoming desired skills in a designer's toolbox. Designers such as Marian Bantjes, Jessica Hische, Sean Wes and Martina Flor, just to name a few, have become not only an inspiration to the rest of us, but also a standard. Their work is not only client-based; they have become their own brand by providing products to their followers as well. Other designers have followed suit, and now it would seem that lettering and calligraphy are everywhere.

Thus, there is growing interest among designers and non-designers to learn. However, the majority of the resources and lessons available are for right-handed people. And when one finds a resource to get started with brush lettering for left-handed people, it might not be as comprehensive. As an educator, I have learned that one of the most challenging aspects for an aspiring left-hand letterer is to apply everything that a right-handed person is teaching. It is almost like doing mental gymnastics.

While I am not able to guarantee your fame and notoriety, I can help you get started with the fundamentals of lettering with the left hand: the position and placement of the arm and wrist, the position of the paper, and holding the tool (brush pens).

What's The Difference?

This last semester, I taught a "special topics" class at the university where I work, titled "Explorations in Lettering and Scripts." There were three students in the class who are left-handed. Since then, I have been trying to gather resources and examples to help them with the practical aspect of the lessons we covered. I have come across several books and blog posts. Some are more scientific than others, and others are more focused on practical tips.

One of the most interesting things I learned while researching for this article is that Dr. M.K. Holder, who is executive director of the Handedness Research Institute, states that writing with the left hand is not simply the opposite of writing with the right hand — nor is it enough to teach the opposite way. The main and most important difference is that, while right-handers write away from the body, left-handers write towards the body. Rest assured, there is hope and many good examples of letterers and calligraphers who are left-handed and who create gorgeous work.

According to some researchers, left-handers account for 10 to 12% of the population. Neal from LeftyFretz, a website for left-handed musicians, has put together a great post reporting the percentage of people who are left-handed, by year and country. Though it varies, there is an overall increase in the percentage of people who self identify as left-handed. However, he states that there is still some stigma about being left-handed. If you are left-handed and are reading this, please know that you are in good company. A great number of famous people were and are left-handed, among them, Alexander the Great, Leonardo da Vinci and Vincent Van Gogh. And according to BuzzFeed, Bruce Willis, Demi Moore, Pierce Brosnan, Bill Clinton, Jim Carrey, David Letterman, Bill Gates, David Bowie, Prince Charles, Prince William and even Barack Obama are all left-handed.

Hand, Wrist And Paper

I grouped these three aspects because they are closely related: the position of the arm and wrist go together with how the paper is positioned. Below you will see several opinions on the matter.
Jodi Christiansen, calligrapher and member of the International Association of Master Penmen, Engrossers, and Teachers of
Handwriting (IAMPETH), writes in her post
"Calligraphy and the Left-Handed Scribe" that there are two types of left-handed ways to hold the pen:

- Curlers curve their hand around the pen to mimic the writing angle that right-handers achieve naturally.

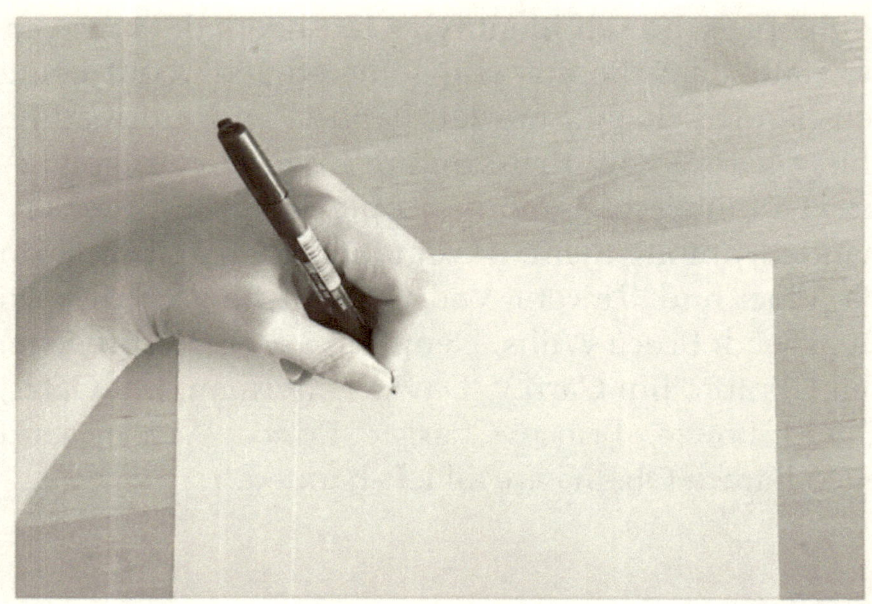

- Non-curlers write without bending their wrist.

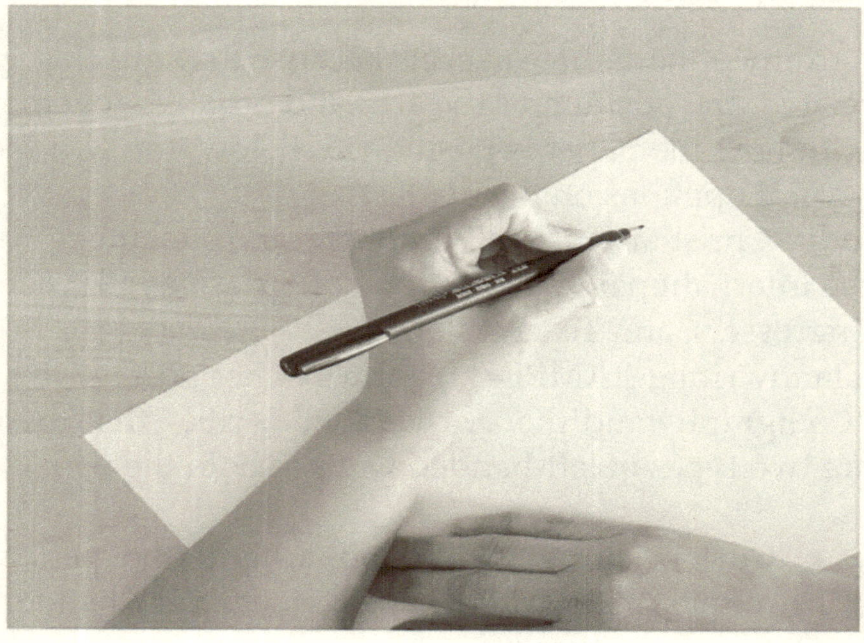

Based on the book, it seems that curlers might have a

harder time doing lettering and calligraphy than non-curlers. The reason for this is that it is hard to see what you've just written. If your hand curls over the line of text you just wrote, it would be difficult to determine how much space to leave, let alone whether the ink is still wet. That would cause a lot of smears.

In addition to Christiansen's hand positions, Jim Bennett, author of the book *Calligraphy for Dummies*, talks about how to position the paper. Bennet lists three positions for the paper:

- It can be held at 45 degrees to the left, making a diamond shape:

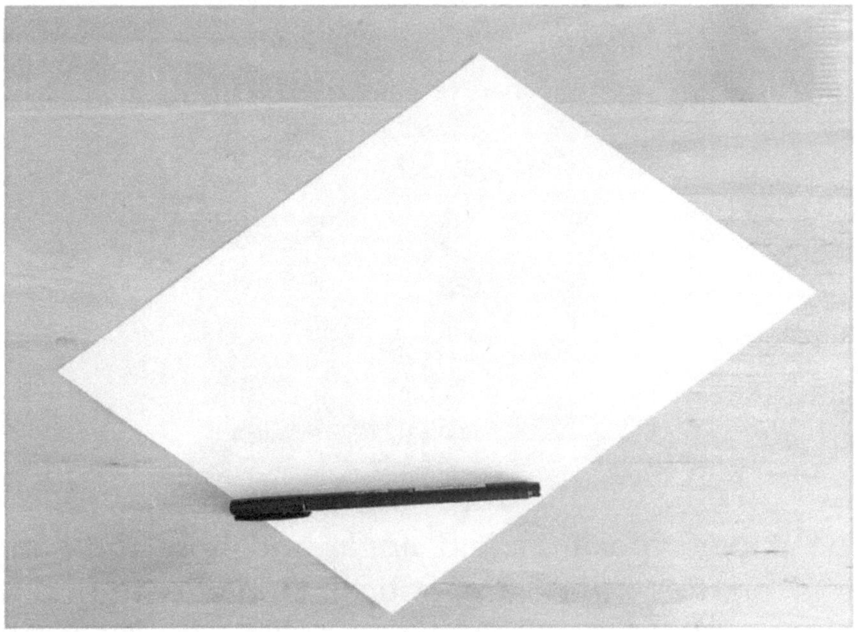

- It can be held at 35 degrees:

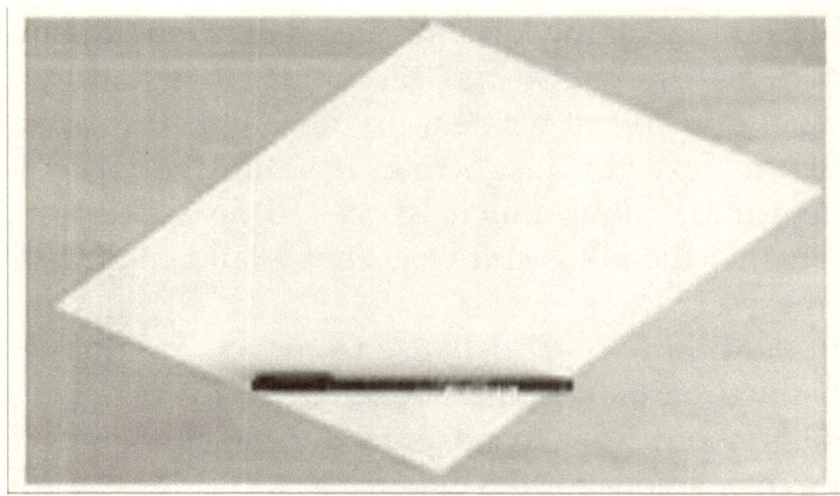

- Or it can be held normally, at 90 degrees:

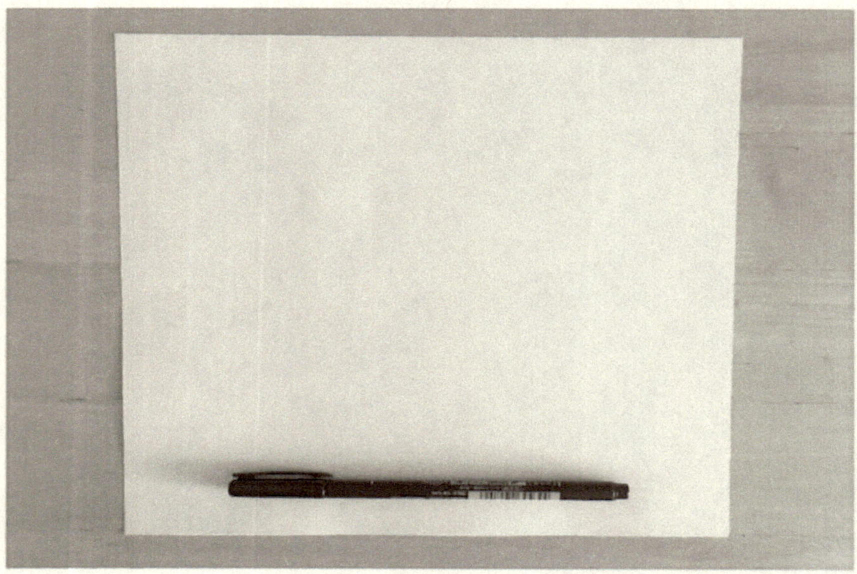

The paper's position and angle and how the hand rests on the paper are critical. Some will find it comfortable to rotate the paper to find the best way to create the letters.

However, Dr. Holder stresses that the best position

for the paper is "to the left of the child's midline, and tilted so that the top right corner of the paper is closer to the child than the top left corner." He explains that this position allows the hand to be positioned "to the left and away from the body at the start of writing line..." He adds that the angle will vary according to the person's preference. However, the most important thing to keep in mind is "to keep the arm perpendicular to the bottom of the page," keeping the wrist straight and "the hand below the writing line."

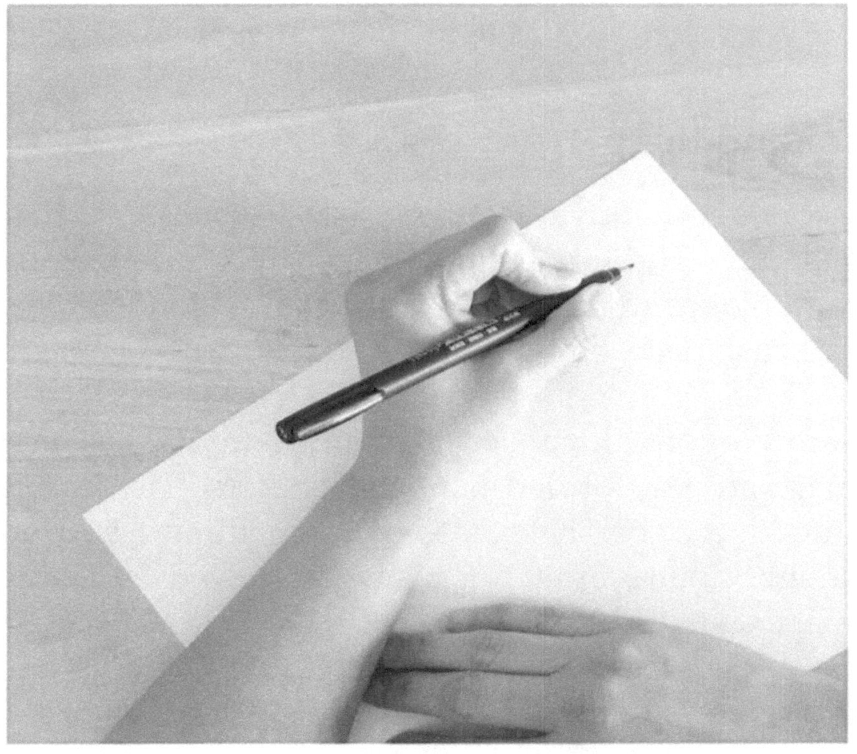

Claire from Heart Handmade UK, who had to relearn

to write after suffering an injury, advises several things and lists a few tools in her article "How to Improve Handwriting Skills for Adults That Are Left Handed." Among these, she advises to try to keep the elbow close to the body, to keep the arm straight, not to curl the wrist and to instead move the paper to a 45-degree angle, which will "automatically bring the hand to the correct writing position."

Below is my student, Talondra, demonstrating how she places the paper. You will notice that she places the paper at approximately a 45-degree angle.

Holding the pen

The biggest advantage of brush pens is their flexibility. The brush tip can turn to the left or the right. Notice in the video below how Talondra holds her brush pen.

Matt Vergotis, logo designer and letterer, has very smart advice for left-handed letterers. He is left-handed, too, but he points out something I had not thought about, in an interview conducted by Daniel Palacios on his blog:

Brush pens have that 360° flexibility to the tip, so they're not like chisel tip pens or calligraphy pens where the nibs split. Those pens are usually suited to specific angles

Even more interesting is that he tends to hold the brush pen above the word. In other words, he tends to curl his hand over the letters. But his top advice is this: repetition. He recommends practicing 15 to 20 minutes a day, and over time you will see improvement.

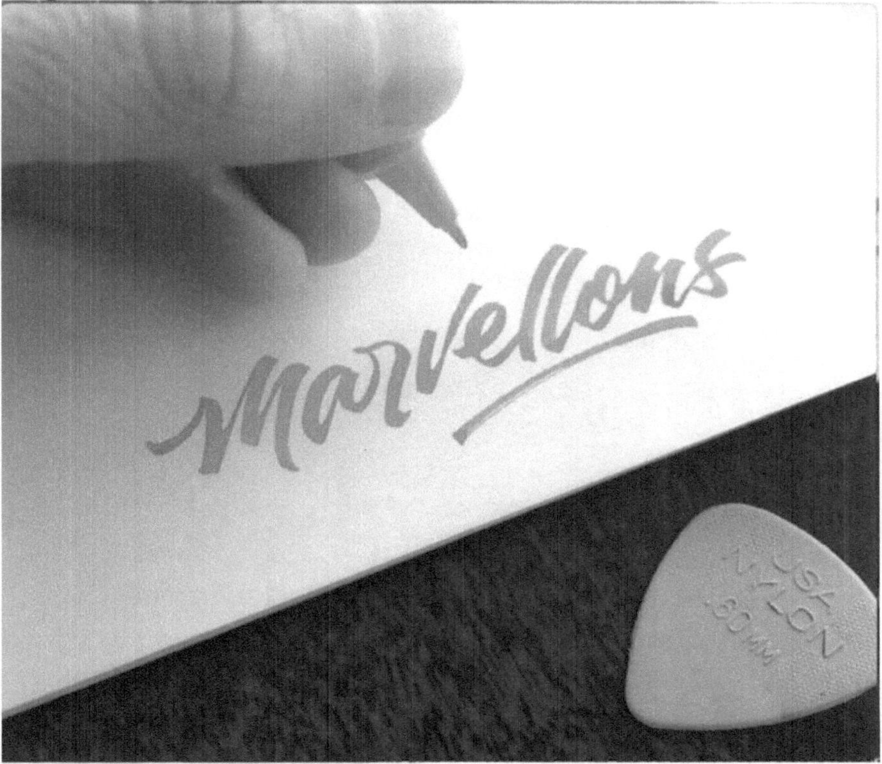

I will add that another element to repetition is patience and a willingness to be comfortable with being uncomfortable. Learning a new skill, no matter how much we like it, will bring moments of discomfort. But it is that patience and determination to overcome the discomfort, which equals deliberate practice, that will help you get better and better.

Talondra, my student, found that the more she practiced, the better she got at making each stroke. When she started, she found that her hand would shake, making her strokes wobbly. Here is a picture of one of her first practice drills:

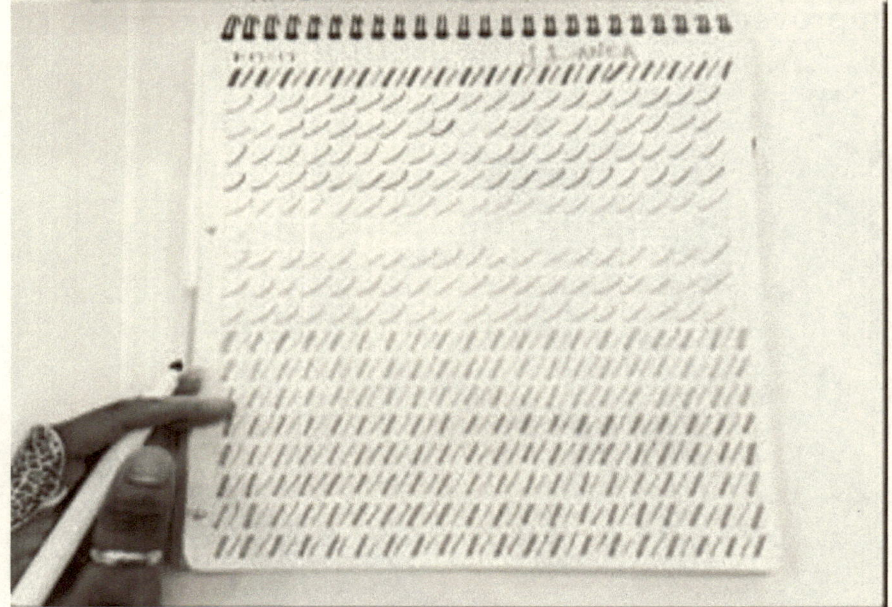

Talondra Keeton's first practice sheet

Eventually, she came up with a unique way to practice the basic strokes that made sense to her. She starts writing on the right side of the page and works her way to the left. I asked her if that is better for her, and she said that, yes, it helps her to control her hand shakiness. Here is a video of the practice:

However, when she writes a word, she starts from

the left and works her way to the right side. Here are two videos of her writing words from two angles:
Notice that she constantly adjusts the pen and the paper to be able to create some strokes. She is very conscious of the contrast there should be between thick and thins, so she tries to accomplish that.
Another useful tip from Dr. Holder is to hold the pen or pencil about 1 inch or 1.5 inches away from the point of the pen or pencil, in order to see what is being written. He stresses that, while the grip might be tight and tense while you're learning it, with time and practice this will improve. Another tip is to write large letters at first, which will help with relaxing the grip, then reducing the size of the letters as one gets more comfortable.

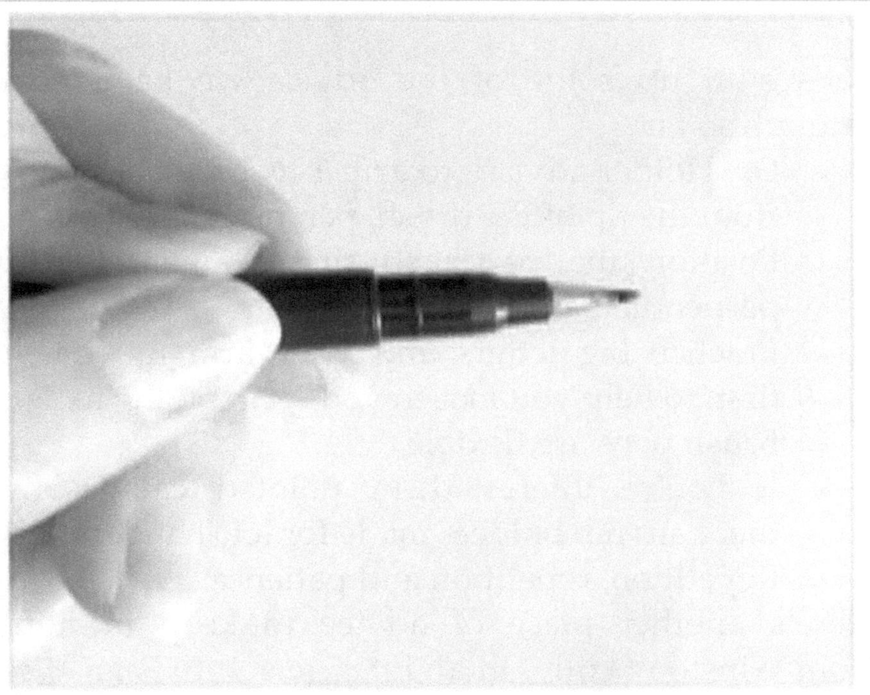

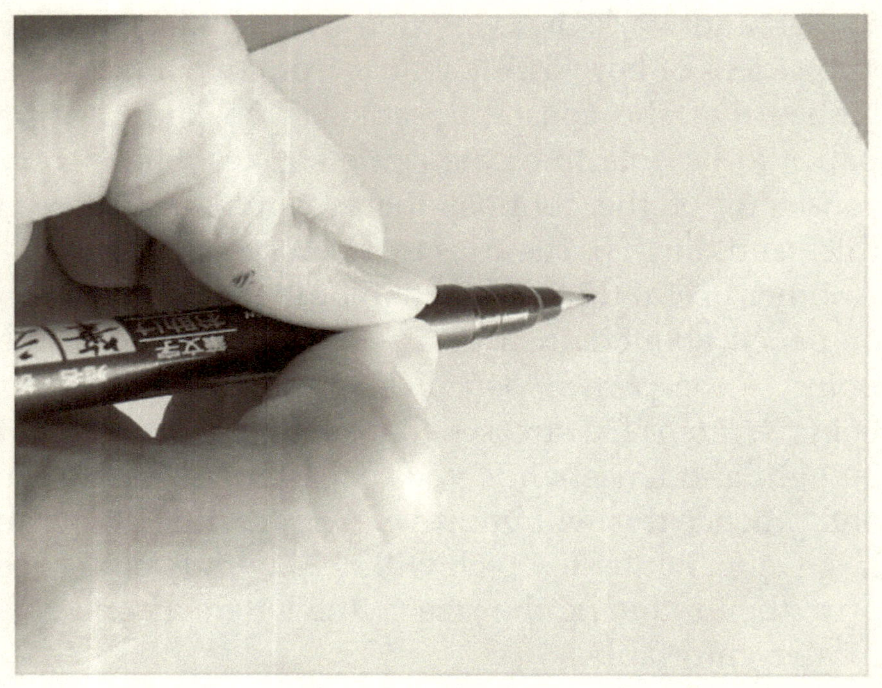

Let's sum up some of the advice we have gone through so far:

- Dr. Holder advises to grip 1 to 1.5 inches away from the tip of the brush, pen or pencil.
- Position the paper so that your arm rests perpendicular to the right side.
- Practice big letters and your arm movement first, to help you loosen your grip on the tools.
- Brush pens are flexible.
- If you're interested in pointed calligraphy, there are nib holders made for left-handers.
- Repetition, repetition and patience.

Here's another piece of advice to keep in mind from Winston Scully, in an interview with Sean Wes:

Let go of the mental barrier. He also has great tips on creating beautiful work, such as start with pencil and then ink the piece; use a grid (parallel lines); and once you get a word where you want it, trace it writing it backwards — he says in the interview that this trains your eye to tackle spacing issues.

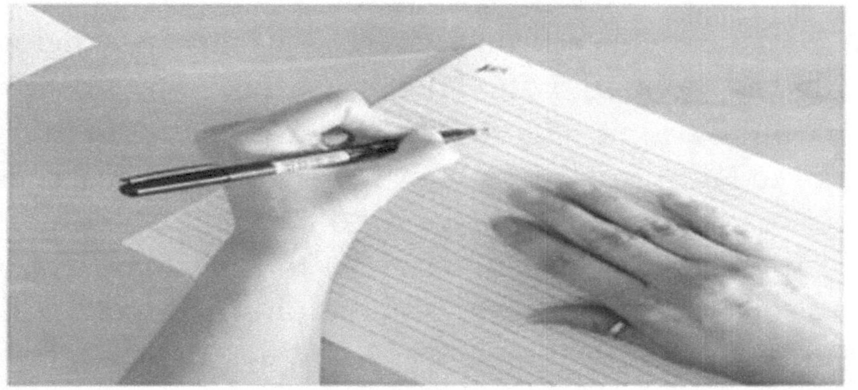

One thing I found very interesting about Talondra's progress is that she taught herself to do some drills without lifting the pen. That alone was a great accomplishment because, as I mentioned earlier, she used to experience a lot of hand shakiness. Take a look at this video of her doing M's:

Lettering is a work in progress, where one moves from larger movement control to smaller movement control. That is why a willingness to fail, to be comfortable with being uncomfortable, and repetitive practice will be your best friends. In the meantime, we can all look at others' work to be inspired to be better.

In this next part, I will list letterers and calligraphers

who are left-handed, for your inspiration. But before we continue, take a moment to think about and practice some of the things you have read here.

Inspiration

In my journey as a brush letterer and now practicing with the pointed pen, I have learned that, before looking at people's work, I have to think about what I want to learn from them. For instance, in this case, as you look at the examples and go to their pages, keep in mind what you have read so far: arm and wrist position, paper position, and holding the pen. Ask yourself some questions:

- How far (more or less) from the point are they holding the brush pen, pencil or pointed pen?
- How are they positioning the paper?
- How are the arm and wrist positioned relative to the paper?
- At what angle do they place the paper and the pen?

Also, keep in mind that unless the person you are looking at teaches, they might have developed a way to work that they are not able to fully explain to you. I mention this because sometimes we all do things by memory, not fully aware of each step we are taking. I have included examples using both the brush pen and the pointed nib.

Ready to see some great work? Here is a list of left-handed calligraphers and letterers.

MATT VERGOTIS

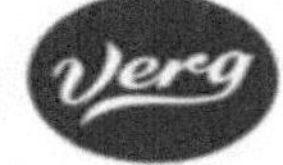

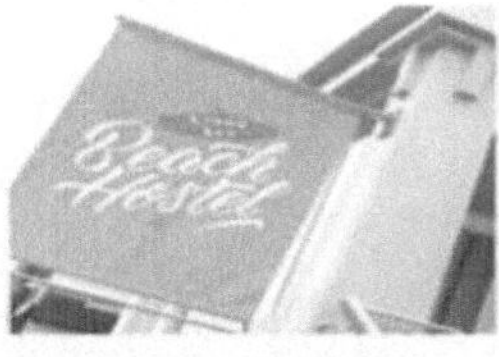

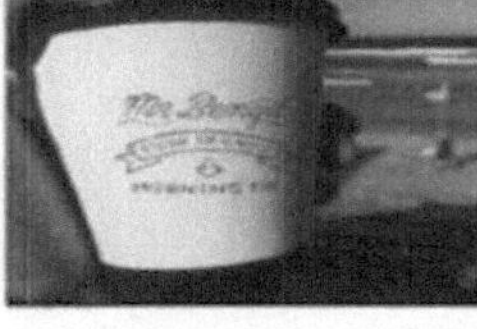

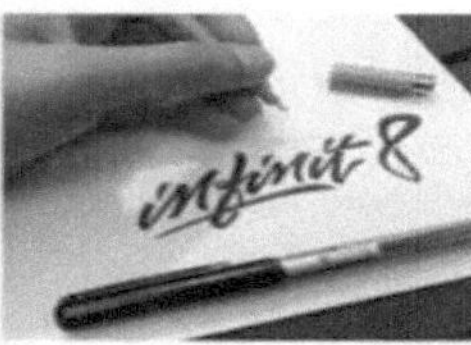

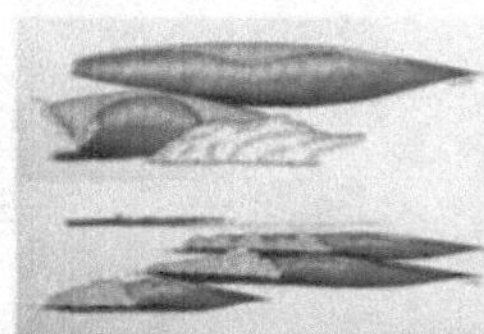

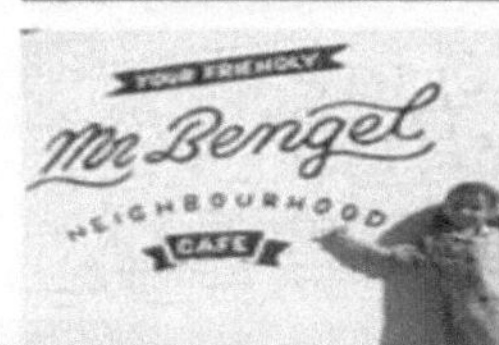

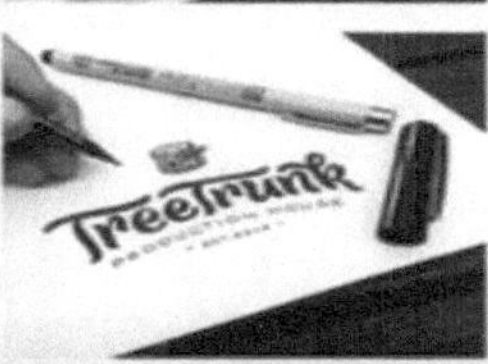

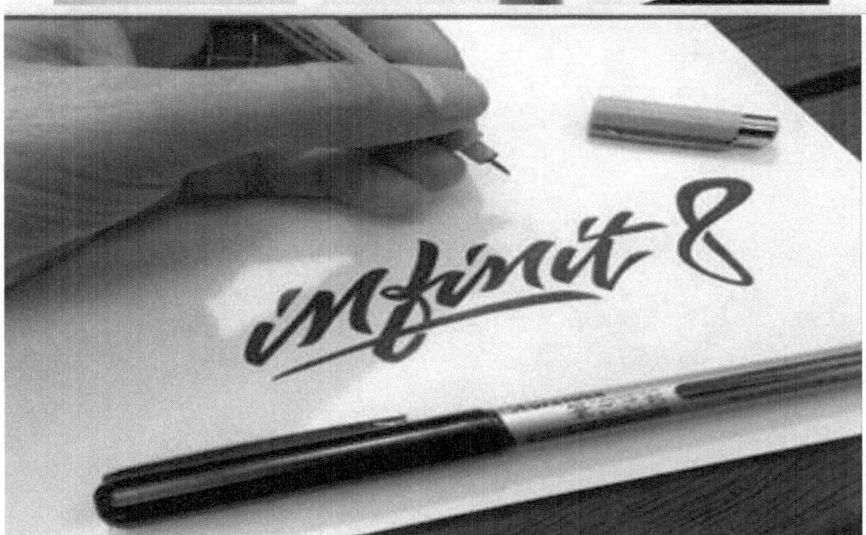

WINSTON SCULLY

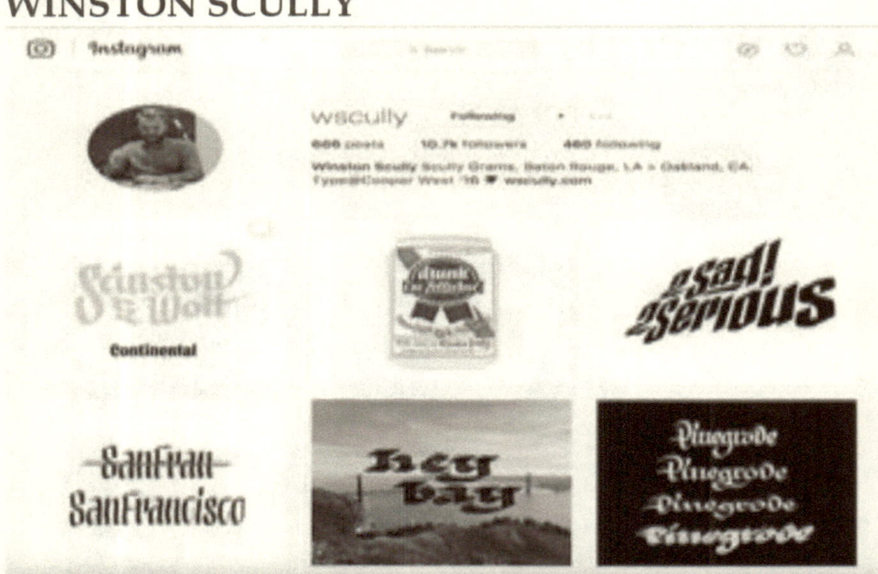

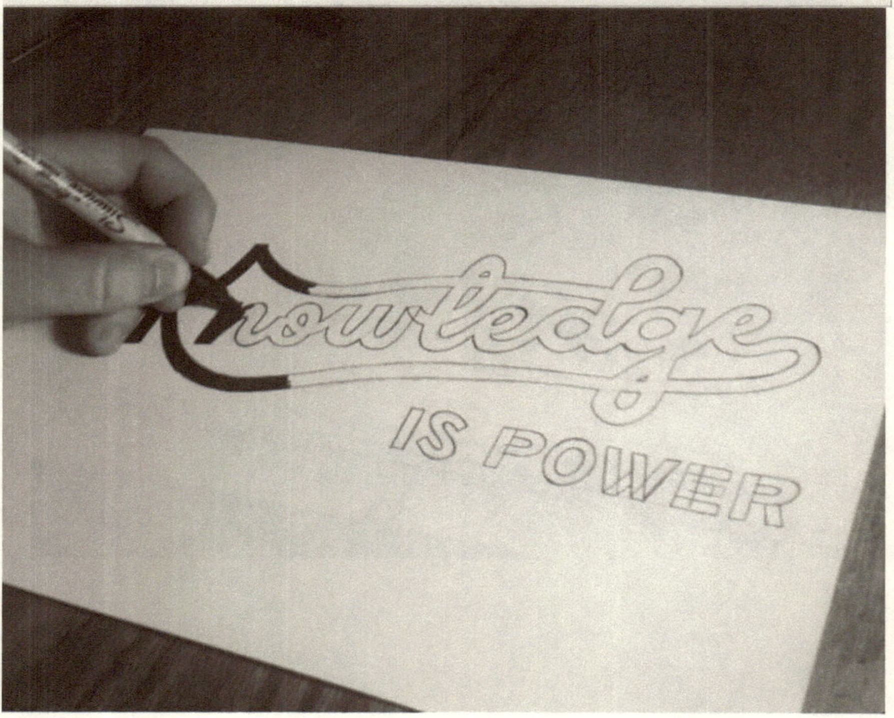

CIARA LEROY

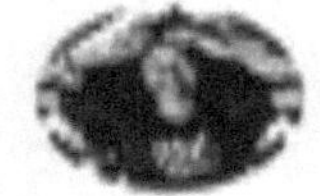

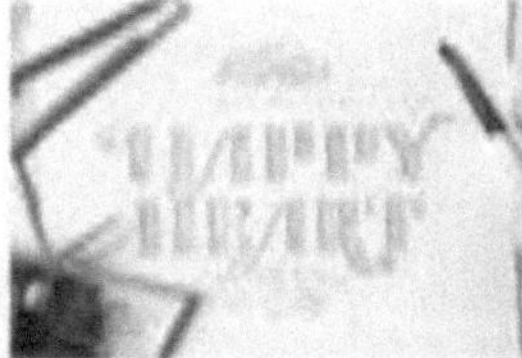

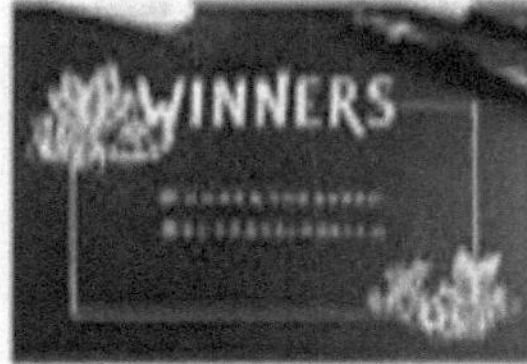
WINNERS

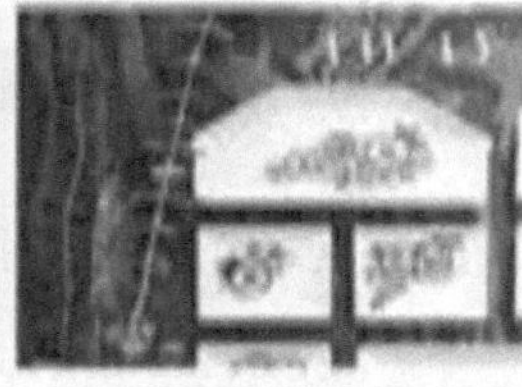

SIT
WITH
US

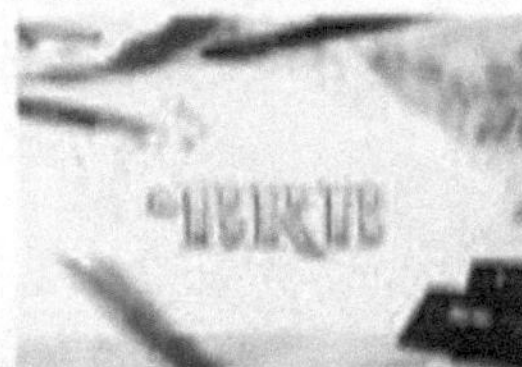

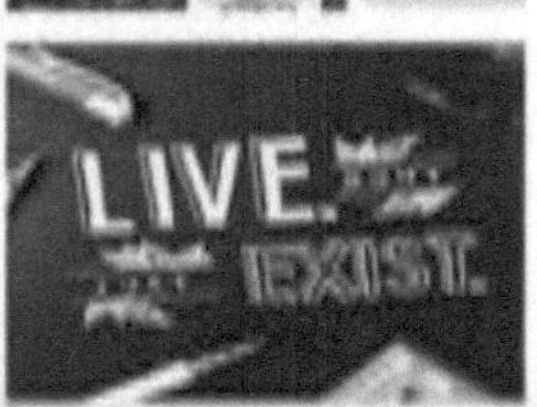
LIVE.
EXIST.

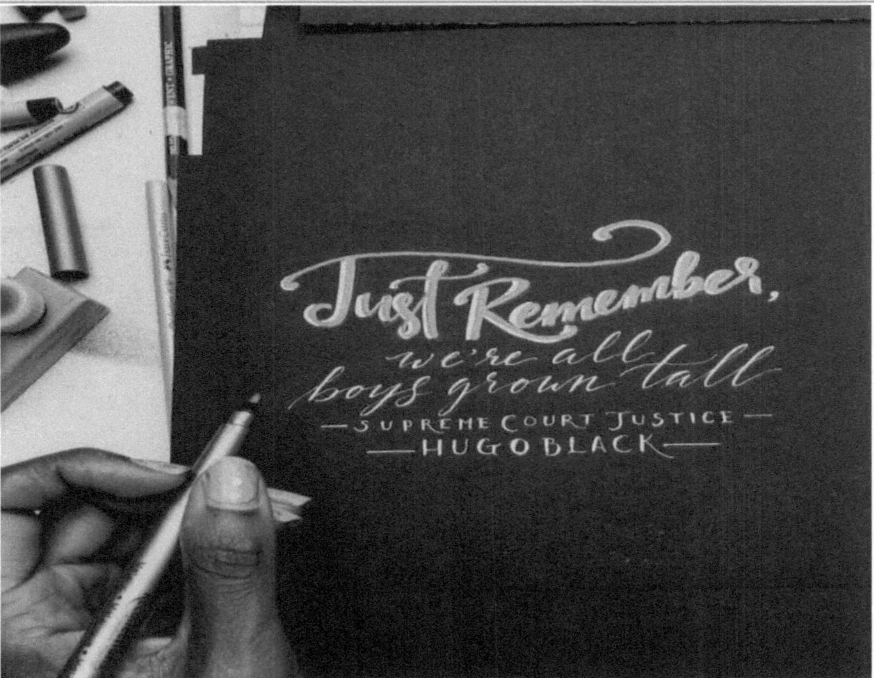
Just Remember,
we're all
boys grown tall
— SUPREME COURT JUSTICE —
— HUGO BLACK —

TARYN NICHOLS

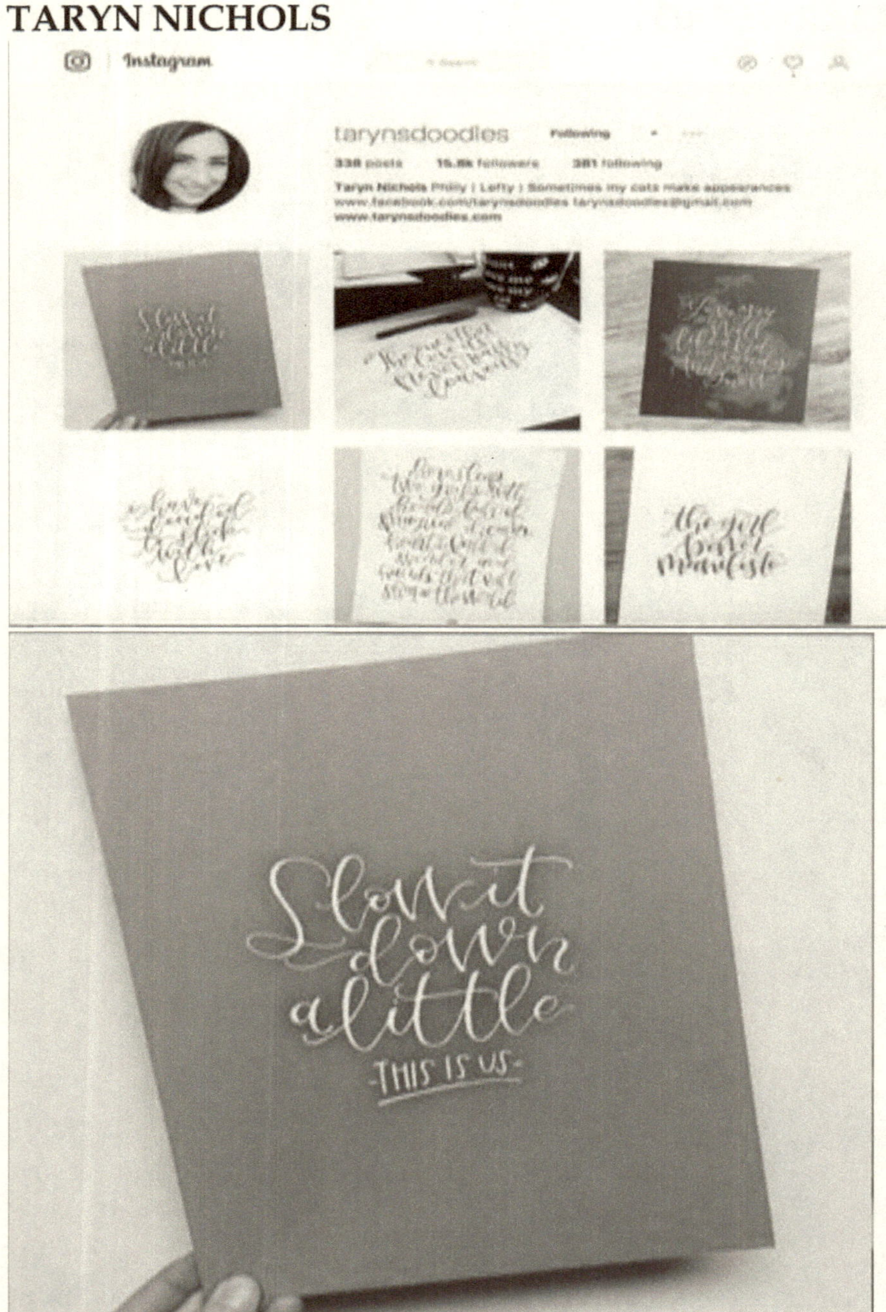

SARAH PEARSON

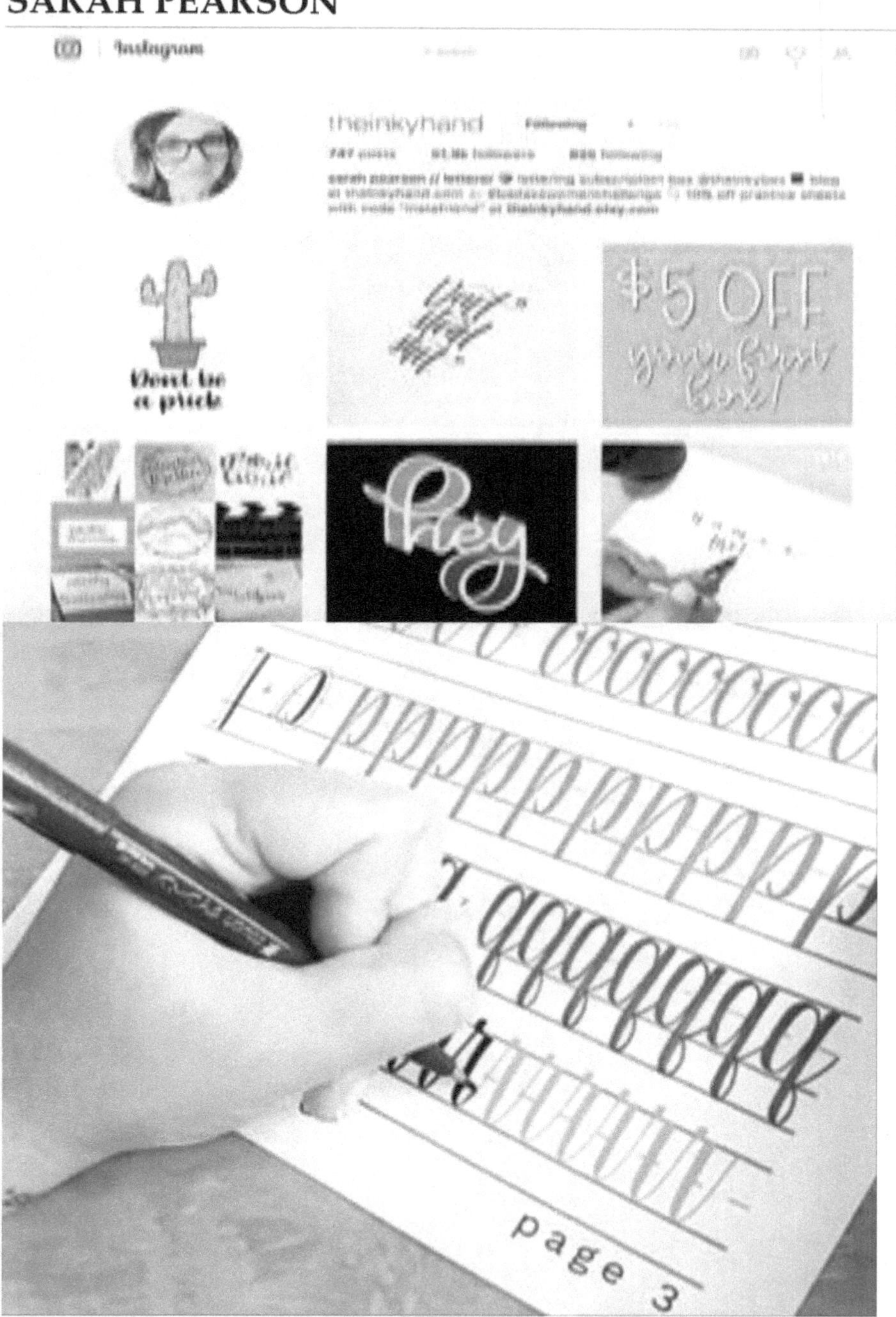

DUTCHLEFTY

Instagram
dutchlefty
27 posts   426 followers   197 following

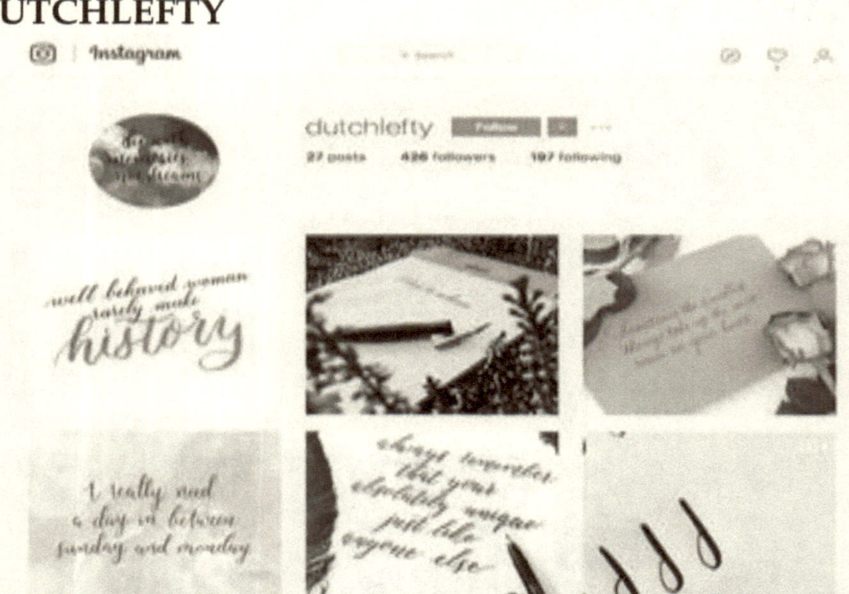

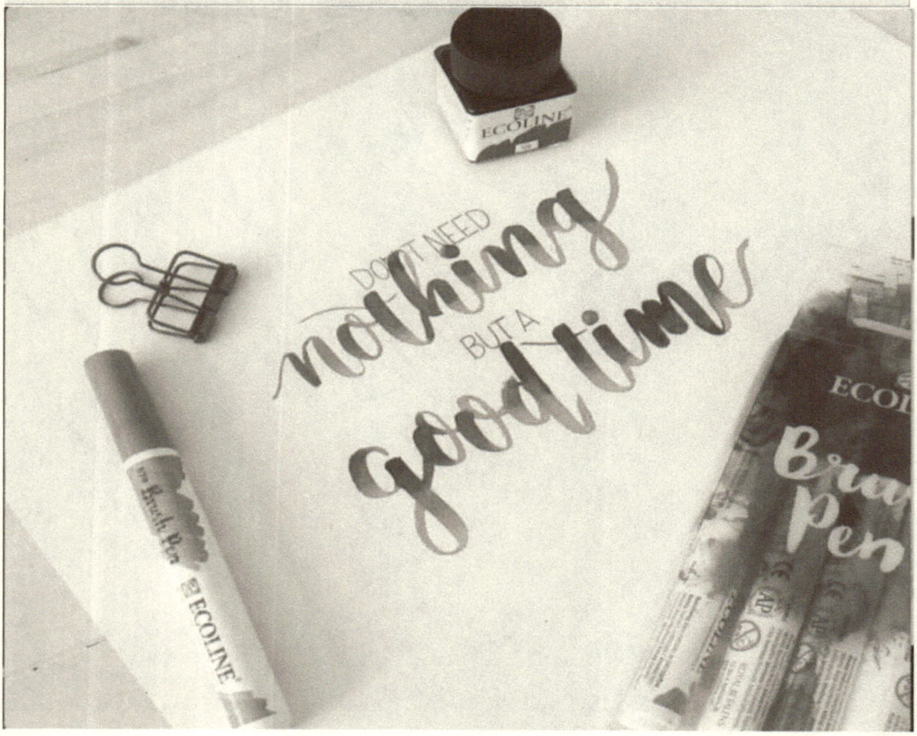

JULIA BROUGHTON

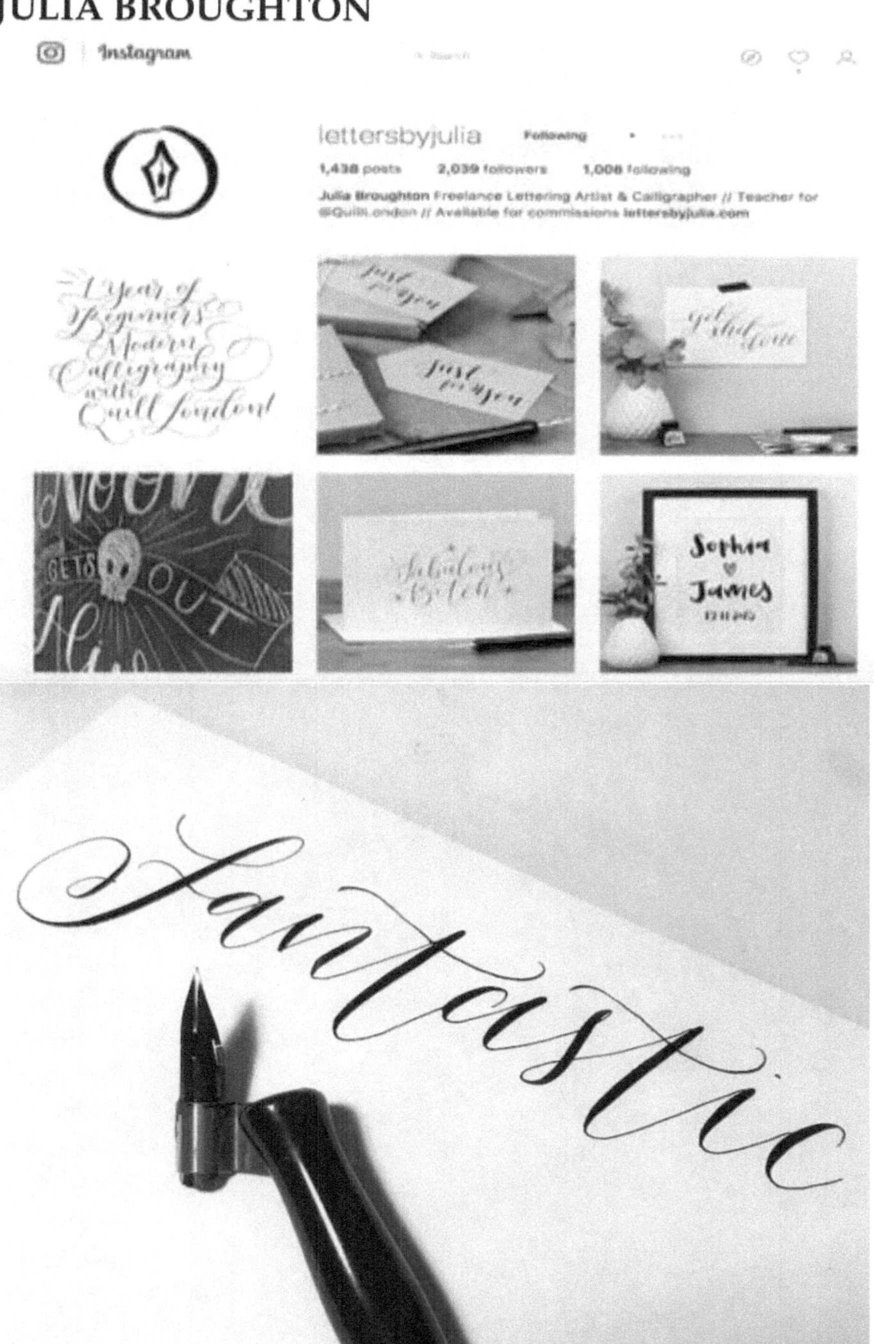

MICHEL D'ANASTASIO

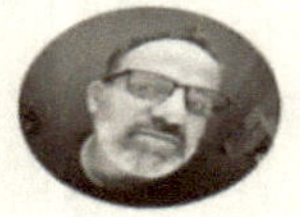

hebrew_calligrapher   Following

812 posts   **2,157** followers   **2,901** following

Michel D'anastasio Modern Jewish Calligrapher from Paris - Israel - New York - Moscou - Tokyo Contact me on contact@script-sign.com
www.script-sign.com

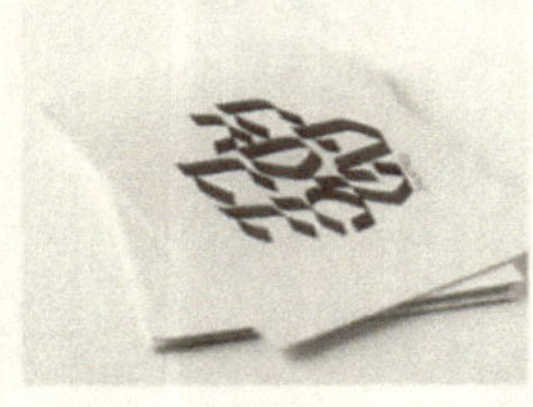 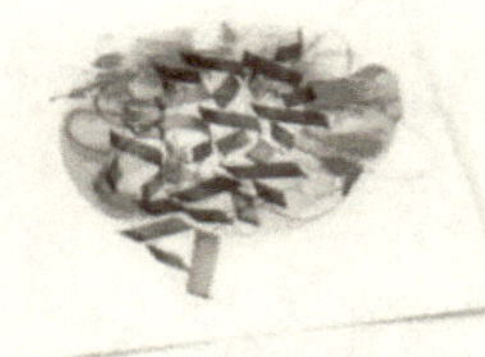 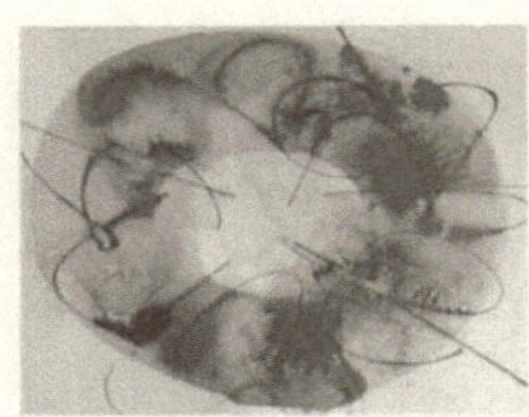

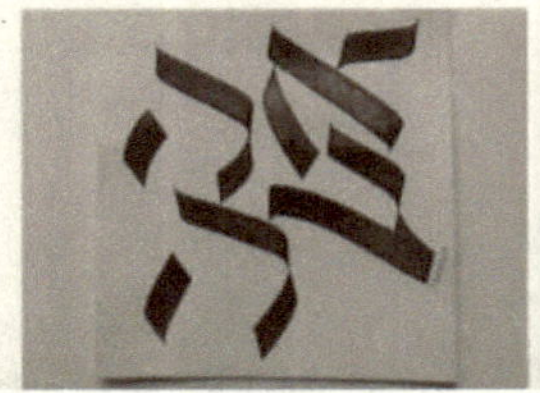 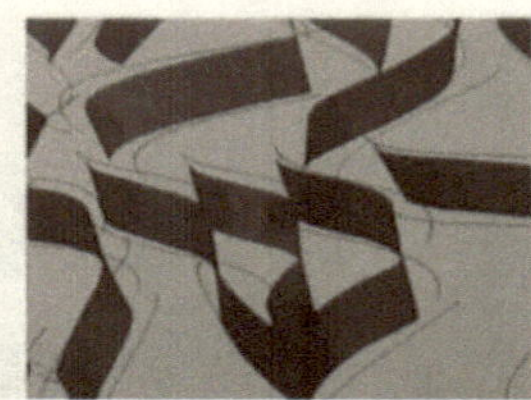 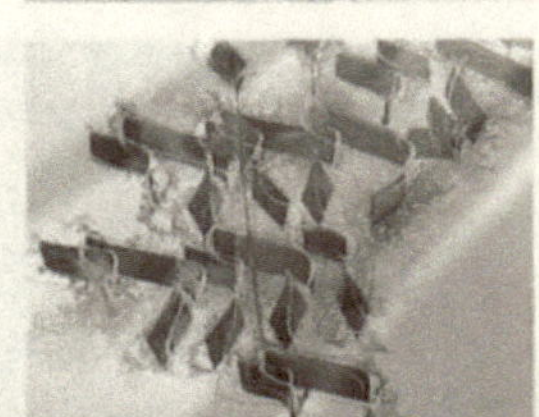

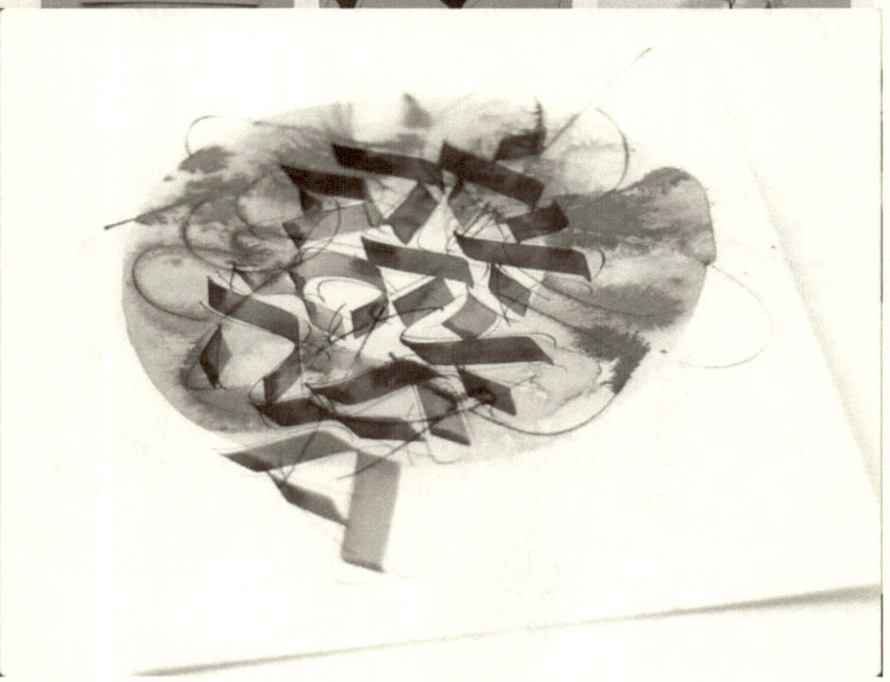

ALYSSA HART

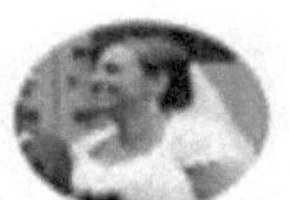
Instagram

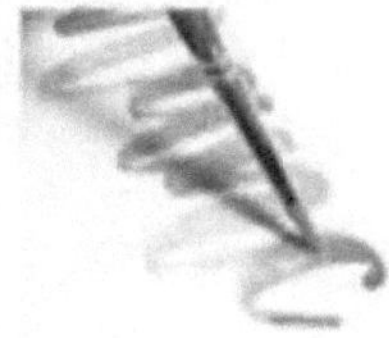

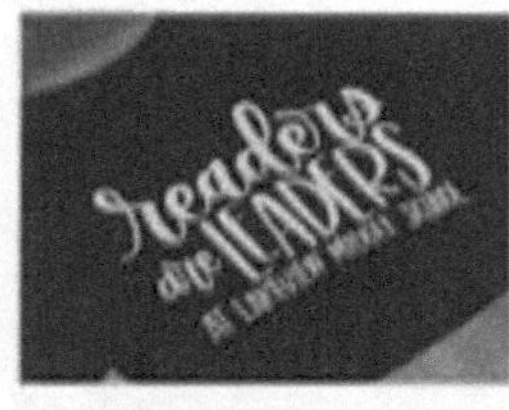

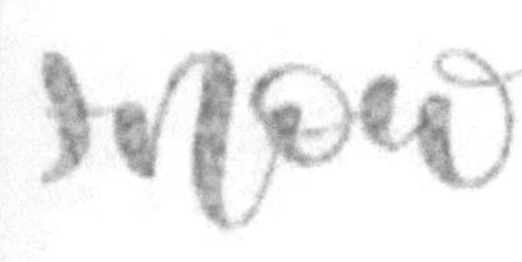
snow

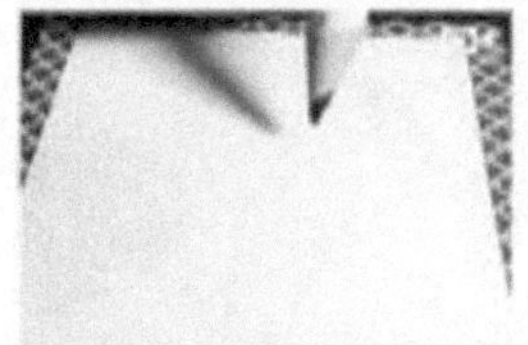

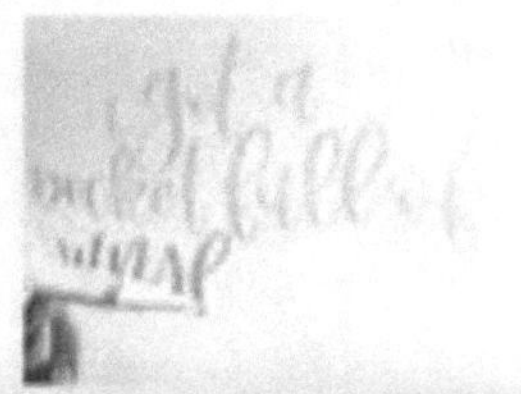

THREE THINGS WILL
LAST FOREVER
faith, hope, & love
AND THE GREATEST
OF THESE IS
love
@happilyeverhart

PAM STEVENSON

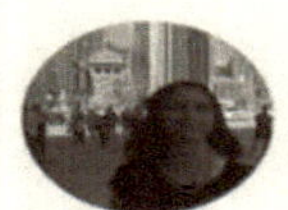

pamcalligraphy Following

241 posts 341 followers 404 following

Pam Stevenson Christ is my savior. Wife, mother of two, graphic designer, left handed calligrapher. Lover of all beautiful things! For commissions, DM me!

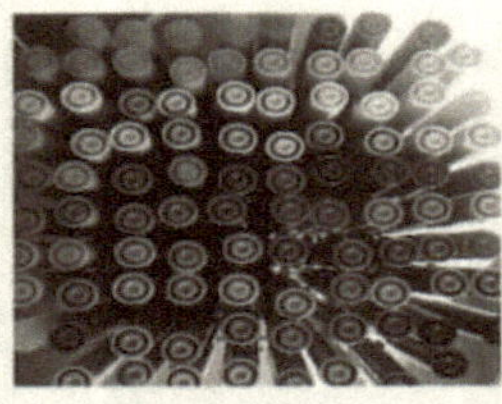

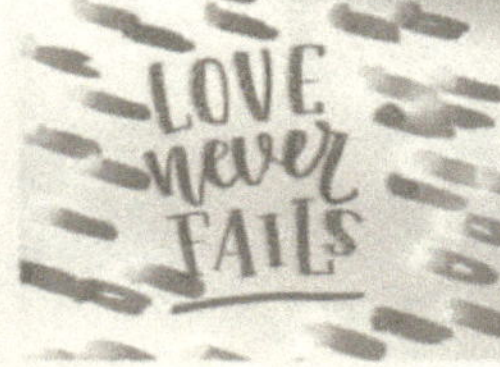

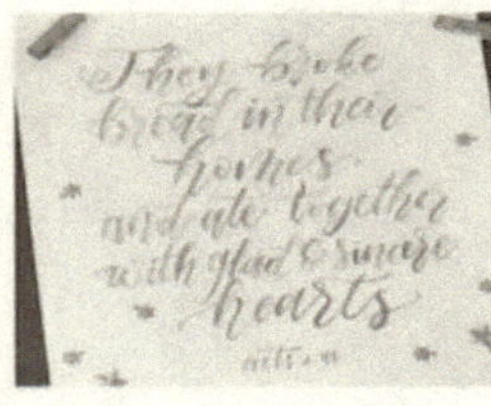

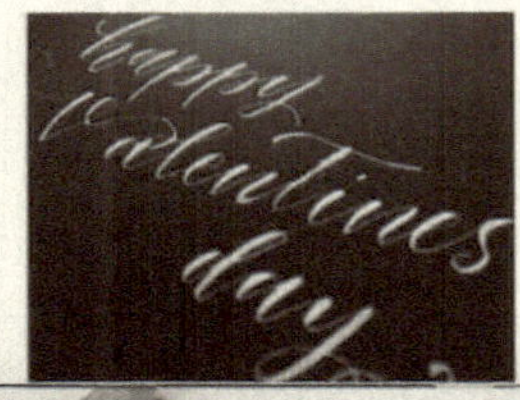

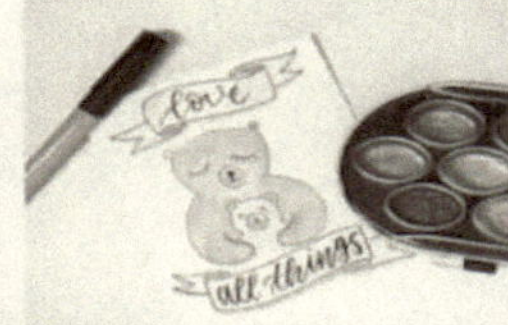

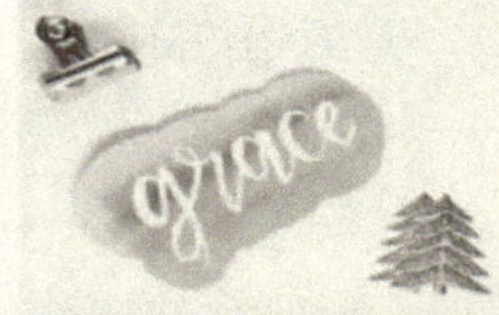

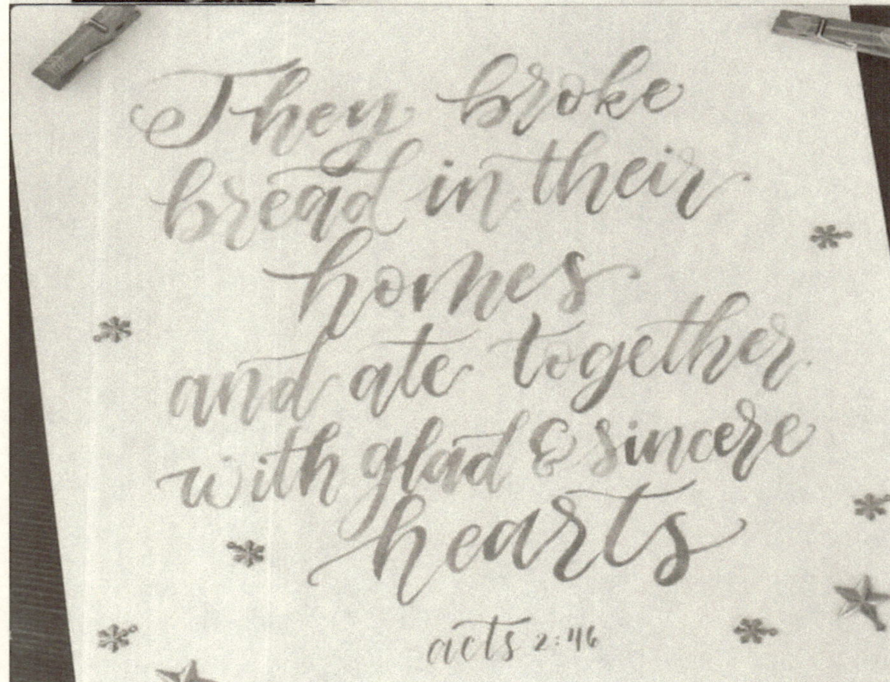

YOUNGHAE CHUNG

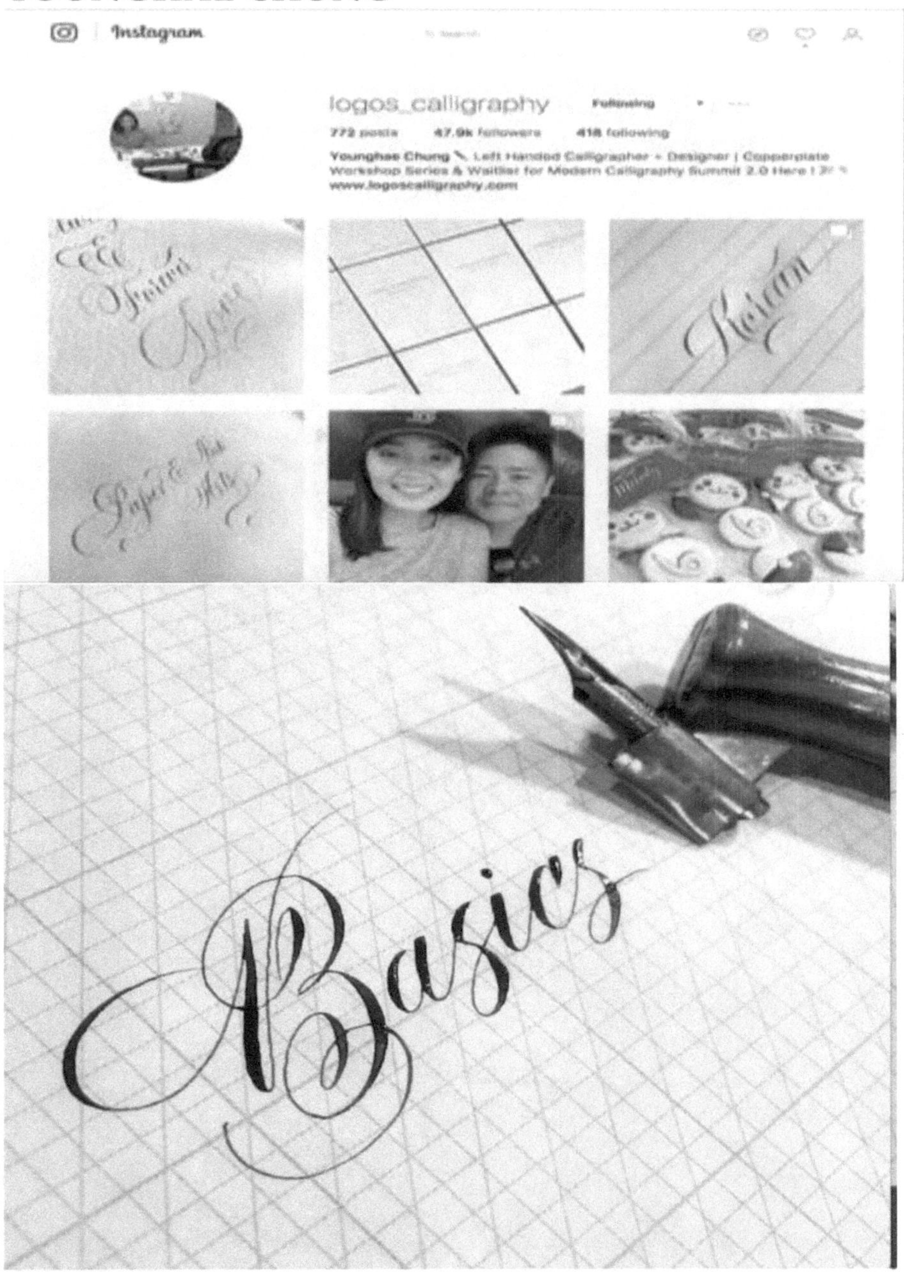

AMANDA HOUSTON

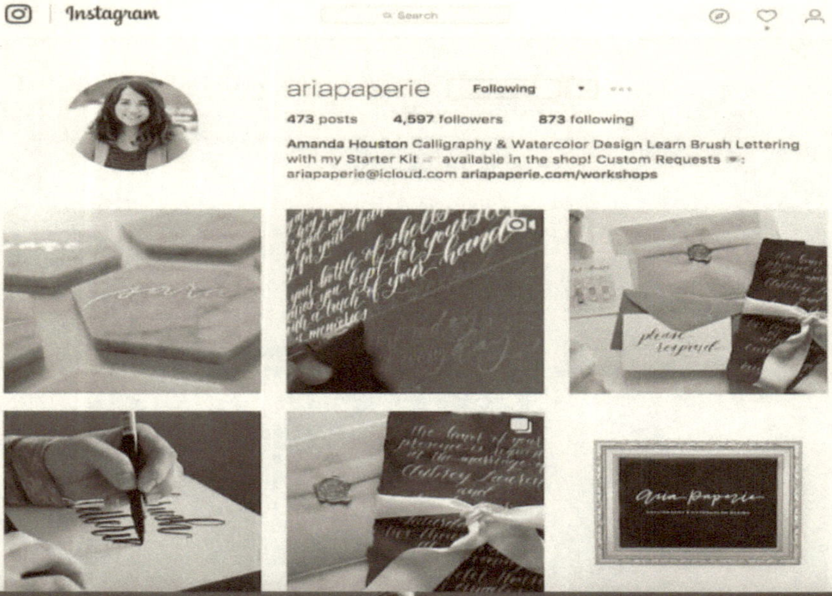

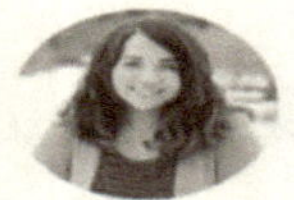

ariapaperie Following

473 posts   4,597 followers   873 following

Amanda Houston Calligraphy & Watercolor Design Learn Brush Lettering with my Starter Kit — available in the shop! Custom Requests ✉:
ariapaperie@icloud.com ariapaperie.com/workshops

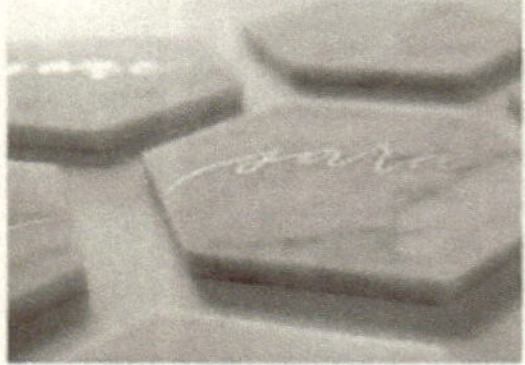
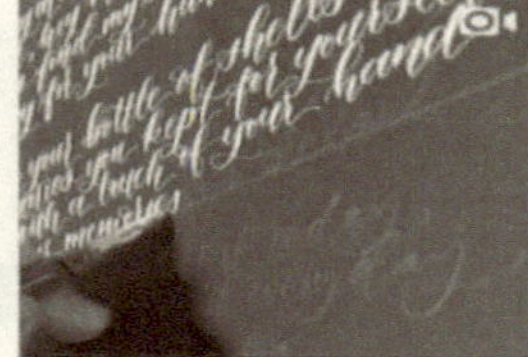
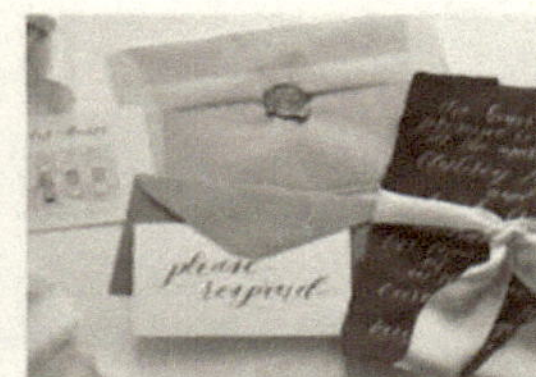
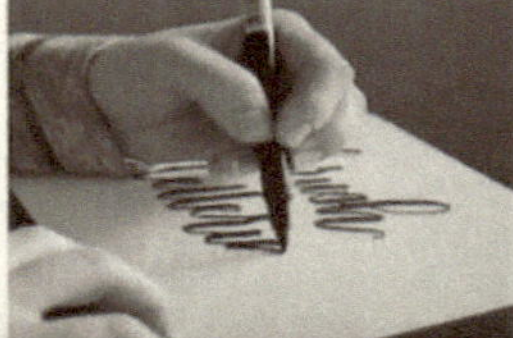
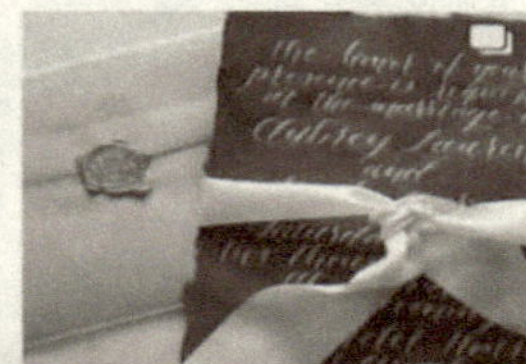

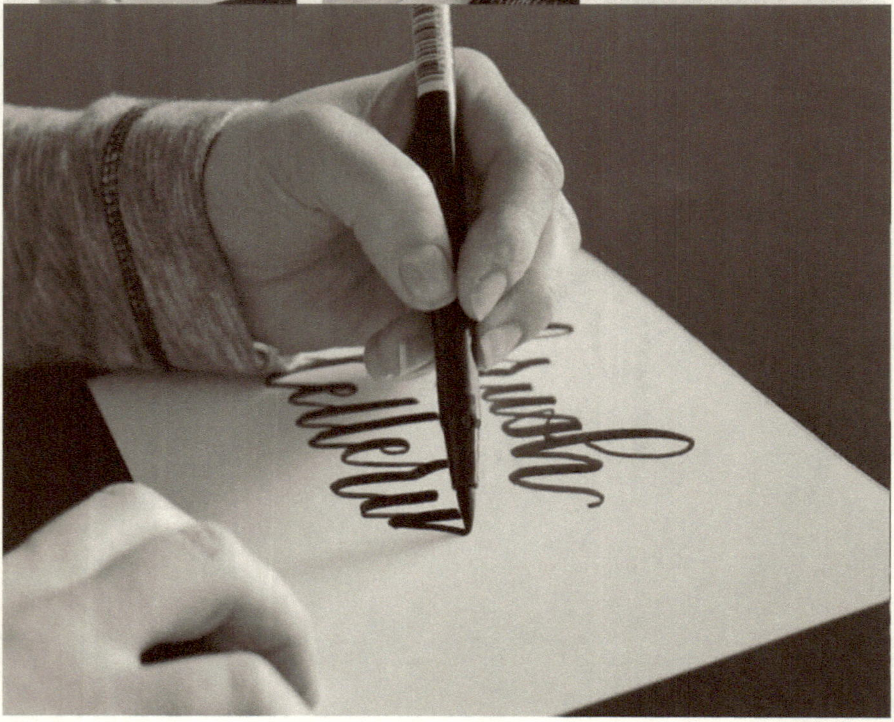

JAVI ALCAZAR

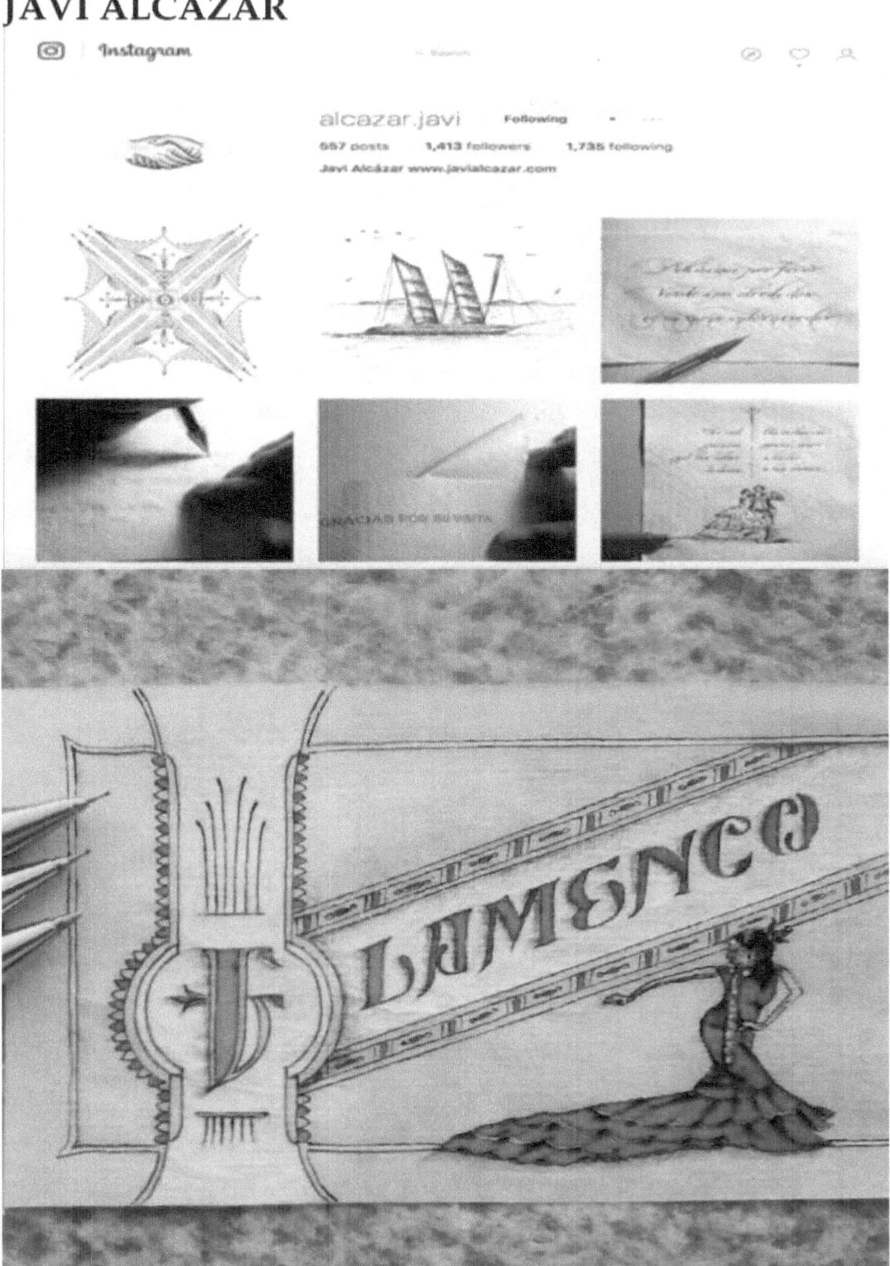

CONCLUSION

Learning lettering is fun, but it can also be a tad frustrating for a number of reasons. Among those reasons, being left-handed in an environment where the majority are right-handed can feel daunting.In this book. I hope you've found tips, practical advice, examples and inspiration. Beyond these, however, I hope you feel that it is attainable and that you can do it.

When I started, I decided to practice every day. Maybe all you have is 15 minutes, or maybe you have more time. What matters is to practice. Maybe you like to learn songs — then use lyrics to practice. Or maybe you like to read books — if so, you can use excerpts to help you practice. Just make sure not to sell another person's excerpts or lyrics. Practicing is OK, but selling it could (and most probably will) get you in trouble.

There are a lot of letterers on Instagram who hold monthly practice challenges. One of my favorites when I started was hosted by Caroline Kelso. Now my favorite is another account named Hand Lettering for Beginners. While you engage in these challenges, keep watching your favorite letterers and calligraphers. Experiment. And have patience. Practice makes progress, and remember: It only gets better with practice! With that in mind, check out my practice sheets here and let me know what you think of them.

www.ingramcontent.com/pod-product-compliance
Lightning Source LLC
Chambersburg PA
CBHW051421130726
47989CB00007B/3018